ollins

Primary Social Studies for Antigua and Barbuda

STUDENT'S BOOK
GRADE 6

T0340554

Anthea S Thomas

William Collins' dream of knowledge for all began with the publication of his first book in 1819.
A self-educated mill worker, he not only enriched millions of lives, but also founded a flourishing publishing house. Today, staying true to this spirit, Collins books are packed with inspiration, innovation and practical expertise. They place you at the centre of a world of possibility and give you exactly what you need to explore it.

Collins. Freedom to teach.

Published by Collins
An imprint of HarperCollins*Publishers*
The News Building
1 London Bridge Street
London
SE1 9GF

HarperCollins*Publishers*
Macken House, 39/40 Mayor Street Upper,
Dublin 1, D01 C9W8, Ireland

Browse the complete Collins catalogue at
www.collins.co.uk

© HarperCollins*Publishers* Limited 2019
Maps © Collins Bartholomew Limited 2019, unless otherwise stated

7

ISBN 978-0-00-832494-0

British Library Cataloguing-in-Publication Data
A catalogue record for this publication is available from the British Library.

Author: Anthea S. Thomas
Commissioning editor: Elaine Higgleton
Development editor: Bruce Nicholson
In-house editors: Caroline Green, Alexandra Wells, Holly Woolnough
Copy editor: Sue Chapple
Proof reader: Jan Schubert
Cover designers: Kevin Robbins and Gordon MacGilp
Cover image: Spillikin/Shutterstock
Typesetter: QBS
Illustrators: QBS and Ann Paganuzzi
Production controller: Sarah Burke
Printed and bound in the UK by Ashford Colour Press Ltd.

Acknowledgements

The publishers wish to thank the following for permission to reproduce photographs. Every effort has been made to trace copyright holders and to obtain their permission for the use of copyright materials. The publishers will gladly receive any information enabling them to rectify any error or omission at the first opportunity.
(t = top, c = centre, b = bottom, l = left, r = right)

p7t Mark Summerfield/Alamy Stock Photo; p7b Studio DMM Photography, Designs & Art/Shutterstock; p16 Mr Pics/Shutterstock; p18 Bill Perry/Shutterstock; p21 Image Courtesy of The Passport Index 2019, PassportIndex.org; p23 RLRRLRLL/Shutterstock; p24 Doomu/Shutterstock; p25 Ververidis Vasilis/Shutterstock; p28 Ralph Eshelman/Shutterstock; p29 EQRoy/Shutterstock; p30t Allstar Picture Library/Alamy Stock Photo; p30b Allstar Picture Library/Alamy Stock Photo; p31l Everett Historical/Shutterstock; p31r Janusz Pienkowski/Shutterstock; p34 Funnyangel/Shutterstock; p35 Naypong Studio/Shutterstock; p36l Timsimages.uk/Shutterstock; p36r Inacio pires/Shutterstock; p37 Doug Armand/Shutterstock; p40 DPRM/Shutterstock; p41l Lindasj22/Shutterstock; p41r Mitja Mithans/Shutterstock; p44l Alter-ego/Shutterstock; p44r Iakov Filimonov/Shutterstock; p45 SCOTTCHAN/Shutterstock; p46 Poring/Shutterstock; p54 Wavebreakmedia/Shutterstock; p55 Pixelheadphoto digitalskillet/Shutterstock; p56 Monkey Business Images/Shutterstock; p57 Monkey Business Images/Shutterstock; p58 Hurst Photo/Shutterstock; p62 Nolte Lourens/Shutterstock; p64 Digitalskillet/Shutterstock; p67 Wavebreakmedia/Shutterstock; p69 Monkey Business Images/Shutterstock; p70 Wavebreakmedia/Shutterstock; p71 Rawpixel.com/Shutterstock; p72 Nopphon_1987/Shutterstock; p73 Petr Jilek/Shutterstock; p74 Wavebreakmedia/Shutterstock.

Contents

Unit 1   Government   4
         What is a government?   4
         The structure of government
         in Antigua and Barbuda   4
         Why is a government
         important?   10
         The electoral process   10
         Stages of the electoral
         process   13
         Systems of government   15
         Systems of government in
         the Caribbean   16
         Good governance   19

Unit 2   Citizenship   21
         Who is a citizen?   21
         Rights and responsibilities
         of a citizen   22
         What makes a good
         citizen?   23
         National and personal
         identity   26
         National heroes   27

Unit 3   Agriculture   32
         Types of industry   32
         What is agriculture?   34
         Agriculture in Antigua
         and Barbuda   35
         Agriculture products that
         Antigua and Barbuda
         exports   36
         Types of agriculture   37
         Agriculture: the positives
         and negatives   42

The impact of globalisation
on agriculture   45
The use of technology in
agriculture   46

Unit 4   Map reading and field
         study   47
         The Caribbean region   47
         Longitude and latitude   49
         Coordinates   50
         Giving direction   51
         The scale   51
         Continents, oceans
         and seas   51
         Physical landforms in
         Antigua and Barbuda   52

Unit 5   Family   53
         What is a family?   53
         Importance of the family   54
         Types of family   54
         Advantages and
         disadvantages
         of different family types   59
         Types of union between
         parents   60
         Family tree   61
         Functions of the family   62
         Roles of family members   65
         Characteristics of good
         parenting   66
         Family problems and social
         issues   70
         Possible solutions   74
         The Rights of the Child   75
         Organisations to promote
         healthy family relationships   76

1 Government

We are learning to:
- define the terms 'government', 'organisation', 'authority', 'laws', 'regulations', 'rules'
- understand the structure of government in Antigua and Barbuda
- understand why government is important
- explain the stages of the electoral process
- identify systems of government, including in the Caribbean
- state what makes a good government.

What is a government?

A government is a group of people who are responsible for running the country. As an organisation, it has the power and authority to manage the country's affairs and to enforce its laws, rules and regulations. In most countries, the government is elected.

Here are some definitions to help with understanding:

- Organisation: a group of people working together to achieve a common goal
- Authority: the power to give orders to other people
- Law: a set of rules that can be enforced by authority
- Rule: a statement of what is allowed
- Regulation: a rule that states how something should be done.

The structure of government in Antigua and Barbuda

There are three branches in the Government of Antigua and Barbuda:

- Legislative
- Judicial
- Executive.

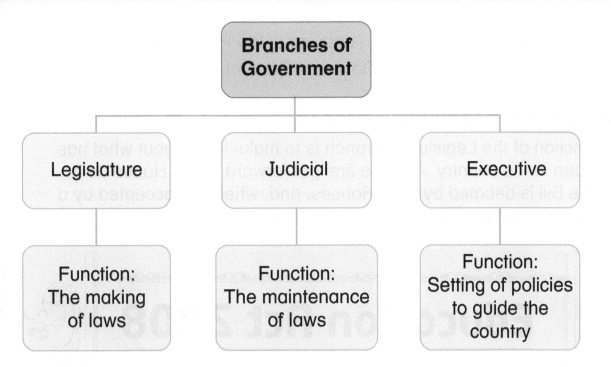

The Legislative branch

There are two Houses in the Legislative branch – the House of Representatives and the Senate.

There are 19 members of the House of Representatives, also known as the Lower House. Seventeen of the members have been elected to represent their constituency and the other two are the Attorney General (responsible for giving legal advice to the Government) and the Speaker of the House (responsible for making sure debates run smoothly).

The House of Representatives has members from the ruling party (the Government) and the opposition party.

The Senate, also known as the Upper House, has 17 members. They are all appointed by the Governor General, mostly on the recommendation of the Prime Minister and the Leader of the Opposition.

Senators are recommended as follows:

- ten on the advice of the Prime Minister
- four on the advice of the Leader of the Opposition
- one on the advice of the Barbuda Council

- one resident of Barbuda on the advice of the Prime Minister
- one by the discretion of the Governor General.

Function of the Legislative branch

The function of the Legislative branch is to make laws about what has to happen in the country. A law is first put forward to the House as a Bill. The Bill is debated by both Houses, and, when it is accepted by a majority, it becomes law. Here is an example of a law:

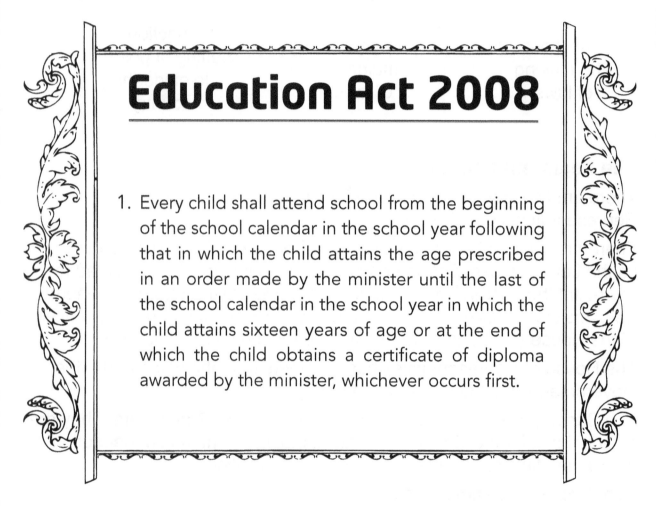

Education Act 2008

1. Every child shall attend school from the beginning of the school calendar in the school year following that in which the child attains the age prescribed in an order made by the minister until the last of the school calendar in the school year in which the child attains sixteen years of age or at the end of which the child obtains a certificate of diploma awarded by the minister, whichever occurs first.

This law says that education is compulsory in Antigua and Barbuda from age 5 to 16 years. This means that every child in Antigua and Barbuda between the ages of 5 to 16 should be in school. Otherwise the parents can be punished for breaking the law.

The House of Representatives meets at the Parliament of Antigua.

The House of Representatives of Antigua – the Parliament building

The members from the Government sit on the left-hand side of the House, while the members of the opposition sit on the right-hand side. The Speaker of the House sits in the centre at the front. A police officer carries in an instrument called a mace to mark the beginning of each session.

An example of a mace

The Executive branch

The Executive branch is made up of members of the Cabinet. The Cabinet consists of the Prime Minister, the Governor General and other ministers of the ruling party. No member from the opposition party is part of the Executive branch.

As leader of the majority party of the House of Representatives, the Prime Minister appoints other members to be their Cabinet ministers.

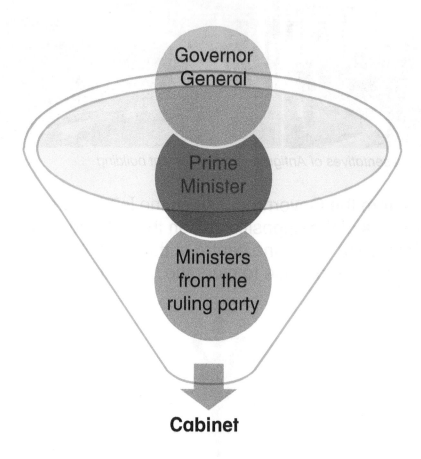

Governor General

Prime Minister

Ministers from the ruling party

Cabinet

Function of the Executive branch

The function of the Executive branch is to carry out the policies set in place by the Legislative branch of government. It also sees to the day-to-day running of the country.

The Cabinet meets once a week, except in an emergency. In order to carry out the policies, the Prime Minister appoints ministers to be head of various ministries. Each ministry is responsible for different aspects of the running of the country. Each minister usually serves until the next general election, but the Prime Minister can change ministers if they choose.

Ministries in Antigua and Barbuda currently include:

- Ministry of Finance and Corporate Governance and Public Private Partnerships
- Ministry of Legal Affairs, Public Safety and Labour
- Ministry of Housing, Lands and Urban Renewal
- Ministry of Public Utilities, Civil Aviation and Energy
- Ministry of Health, Wellness and The Environment
- Ministry of Sports, Culture, National Festivals and the Arts
- Ministry of Foreign Affairs, Immigration and Trade
- Ministry of Social Transformation, Human Resource Development, Youth and Gender Affairs
- Ministry of Tourism and Investment
- Ministry of Information, Broadcasting, Telecommunications and Information Technology
- Ministry of Education, Science and Technology
- Ministry of Works
- Ministry of Agriculture, Fisheries and Barbuda Affairs

Sometimes the Prime Minister may decide to reorganise, and perhaps rename, the ministries.

The Judicial branch and its function

This is the branch of government that ensures that laws are interpreted and applied fairly. It is done through the court system, which decides whether a person accused of breaking the law is innocent or guilty.

The Judicial branch – also known as the Judiciary – is independent of the other two branches, although magistrates are appointed by the Attorney General in the Executive. The Judiciary consists of the Magistrates Court for minor offences and the High Court for major offences.

After going to the High Court, a case can be referred on appeal to the Organisation of Eastern Caribbean States (OECS) Supreme Court. The final court of appeal is the Privy Council, in London.

Why is a government important?

A government runs a country on behalf of all the citizens, the people who live in it. Without government and laws, it would not be possible to maintain order. Government protects its people from harm as well.

For example, consider the rules in your own home. *What rules do you have to follow? Why did your parents make these rules?* The rules are there to make the home run smoothly and to protect you from harm.

The citizens of a country pay their taxes and in return the government provides services for the citizens, such as the police, schools and roads.

The electoral process

A constituency is an area in a country where voters elect a representative to a local or national government. An election is the process during which voters choose candidates by voting for them. A candidate is a person who seeks election.

In Antigua and Barbuda there are 17 constituencies. Antigua is divided into 16 constituencies and Barbuda is considered to be one constituency. Each constituency has candidates who would like to win an election so that they can represent the people in the government.

This map shows all the constituencies in Antigua and Barbuda.

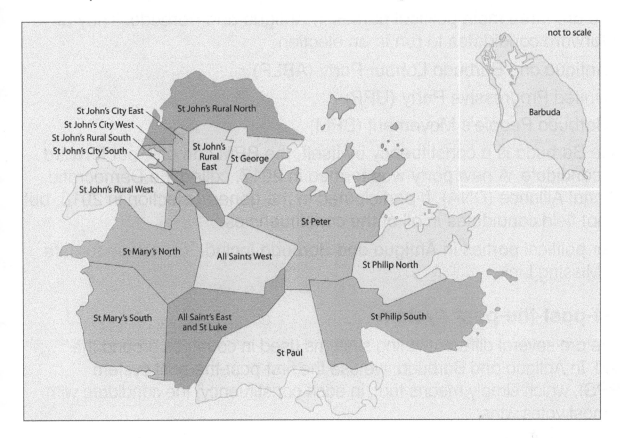

Elections are held once every five years in Antigua and Barbuda. The last election was held on 21 March 2018, so the next election is scheduled for 2023.

Who can vote?

To be able to vote in an election you must be:

- aged 18 years or over
- a legal citizen or resident of the country
- a registered voter with a voter's ID card.

Voting is important and a voter needs to think hard about who will represent them the best, in order to decide who to vote for. People also often vote for the candidate from a particular political party – the party that they think will run the country well.

Major political parties in Antigua and Barbuda

There are three main political parties in Antigua and Barbuda. They all put forward candidates to run in an election:

- Antigua and Barbuda Labour Party (ABLP)
- United Progressive Party (UPP)
- Barbuda People's Movement (BPM)

Since Barbuda is a constituency by itself, the BPM can only put forward one candidate. A new party was formed in 2017, called the Democratic National Alliance (DNA). It participated in the general election in 2018, but did not field candidates in all of the constituencies.

Other political parties in Antigua and Barbuda include Go Green for Life and Missing Link.

First-past-the-post system

There are several different voting systems used in countries around the world. In Antigua and Barbuda, we use the first-past-the-post system (FPPS), which simply means that, in each constituency, the candidate with the most votes wins.

This is how the system works, in order to form a government:

- Each constituency provides one person to sit in the House of Representatives. (This is called a seat.)
- The constituency is contested by one candidate from each political party. (Independent candidates can stand for election, too.)
- People vote for the candidate they choose. They do not vote directly for a party, although their choice of candidate to vote for might be affected by which party the candidate belongs to.
- The party that wins the most seats forms the government of the country.

Stages of the electoral process

Here are the key stages of the electoral process.

1. The election is announced by the Prime Minister.
2. The Governor General dissolves (formally ends) Parliament by issuing a writ of election. The election must be held within 90 days.
3. The political parties choose the candidate they would like to represent them in each constituency. Independent candidates may also stand for election – they do not belong to any political party. On Nomination Day, the official candidates are confirmed if they have ten nominations and their names will go on the ballot paper. A ballot paper is the piece of paper where voters record their vote.
4. Each candidate pays a fee of $500.00. If they receive one third or more of the votes, the fee is refunded.
5. Campaigning for the election begins. The candidates and their supporters go door to door trying to persuade people to vote for them. There are adverts in the media – on radio, television and in the newspapers – and there are public rallies.
6. Election day: the people vote for the candidates of their choice.
7. The winners are declared.

How do people vote?

On election day, people go to their polling station to vote. They are told which polling station they must go to. Polling stations open at different times in different countries. For example, in Antigua and Barbuda they are open from 6 a.m. to 6 p.m. and in Dominica the times are 7 a.m. to 5 p.m. Voters can cast their vote at any time during those hours.

This diagram shows you what happens inside a polling station.

Voter enter the polling station, states name, address and occupation and presents ID card

Voter's name is found in the register by the poll clerk

The voter is then directed to the presiding officer who, having been satisfied as to the identity of the voter, issues a ballot paper placing the official mark on the bottom right-hand/left-hand corner of the ballot paper.

Voter proceeds behind compartment, marks their ballot and folds it to conceal their vote

The voter shows the back of the ballot paper to the presiding officer to verify the official mark they had earlier placed on the ballot paper

The voter then dips the finger nearest to the thumb on the right hand in black electoral ink. The ballot is then placed in the ballot box and the voter leaves the station

The person responsible for the election and the count is known as the Returning Officer.

Each polling district is managed by the Returning Officer who has a presiding officer and several poll clerks working with them in each polling district. There are also scrutineers or agents who works on behalf of their respective political party.

When the polling station closes, the ballot papers are taken to a central place in each constituency, where they are counted.

The results for each constituency are announced by the Returning Officer.

The entire election is conducted by the Antigua and Barbuda Electoral Commission (ABEC).

Characteristics of a good candidate

There are certain characteristics that improve a candidate's chances of being elected. These include:

- having a high moral standard
- being honest
- having compassion
- having a good working knowledge of the issues affecting their constituency
- having not been in trouble with the law
- being an upstanding citizen.

Systems of government

There are a number of different types of government. These include:

- democracy
- autocracy
- monarchy.

Democracy

In a democracy, a country's citizens choose their government by voting for them in elections. Most Caribbean countries are democracies.

Here are the basic principles of a democracy:

- The key principles are fairness, justice and respect for others.
- There should be respect for the law, for human rights and for civil liberties.
- There should be free and fair elections to choose a government.
- The people who are elected to serve should do so with honour and be held accountable for what they do.

Autocracy

Autocracy is a system of government in which the power and authority to rule lie in the hands of a single person. There are several forms of autocracy, including military dictatorship and absolute monarchy. Criticism is usually forbidden.

Monarchy

A monarchy is a country with a king or queen as head of state. These days, the king or queen has very little real power. Some countries in the Caribbean are parliamentary monarchies. For example, Barbados is a parliamentary monarchy because it has a parliament and a monarch as the head of state. A monarchy is a system where a state can be headed by a monarch or sovereign. This is usually for as long as the monarch lives.

Systems of government in the Caribbean

There are two main types of government in the Caribbean: constitutional monarchy and republic.

Constitutional monarchy

Countries with a constitutional monarchy have a king or queen as their official head of state, but the monarch has very little power, if any. All the authority lies with the constitution. A constitution is the principles and laws by which a country is governed.

Antigua and Barbuda is a constitutional monarchy, with the monarch being Queen Elizabeth II. She does not make any decisions as to how the country is run or governed. The power lies in the constitution of Antigua and Barbuda.

The people use the democratic process to choose who they want to govern them. The leader is the Prime Minister, and the Governor General is the official representative of the Queen.

Many of the countries of the Caribbean who were once ruled by the British have a constitutional monarchy system of government.

Republic

A republic is a system of government where there is no monarch. Instead, there is a head of state who is chosen by the people in an election.

There are two types of republic:

- A **presidential republic**, where the head of state is also the head of government. The president has full constitutional powers. An example of this type of republic is Guyana.

- A **parliamentary republic**, where the head of state is ceremonial only and the Prime Minister is the head of government. As a result, the Prime Minister has executive authority. Trinidad and Tobago and the Commonwealth of Dominica have this system and the presidents have limited power.

The Westminster system of government

A Parliamentary System of Government

No single person has supremacy over others in policy or decision-making in a parliamentary system. A Prime Minister cannot force their own ideas over their own party, much less the whole parliament itself because **Prime Ministers are purely first among equals** within parliament.

Vested interests need to individually influence and pressure a majority of members of parliament. Hence, it is extremely expensive and difficult for influence-peddlars and vested-interest groups to influence or control policy.

Head of State
(Ceremonial President or Ceremonial Monarch)
No real decision-making or policy-making powers.

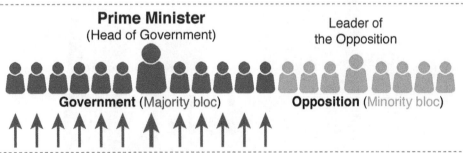

Parliament

Executive and Legislative Branch

Prime Minister
(Head of Government)

Leader of the Opposition

Government (Majority bloc)   **Opposition** (Minority bloc)

The Westminster system is a democratic system of government based on the system of the United Kingdom. It is used in a number of Caribbean countries, including Antigua and Barbuda.

Features of the Westminster system

- A head of state whose duties mainly consist of performing the role of a ceremonial figurehead, for example, Governor General president or monarch.
- A head of government known as the Prime Minister, who is the leader of the largest party in Parliament.
- An Executive branch that is headed by the Prime Minister and his or her cabinet.
- Parliamentary opposition, in the form of the second largest party in Parliament.
- An elected legislature, often with a lower and upper house where the lower house is elected. This is the House of Representatives in Antigua.
- The lower house can dismiss a government by winning a vote of no confidence.
- Parliament can be dissolved and an election called at any time.
- Parliamentary privilege which allows the legislature to discuss any issue without fear. (Immunity as to what is being said.)

The Houses of Parliament in Westminster, United Kingdom, which gives its name to the Westminster system of government

Good governance

When we talk about 'governance', we are referring to the way that a country is governed. Good governance depends on a number of factors:

- The citizens help decide how the country is run through voting and understanding the political system of the country.
- The judicial system is independent and fair.
- The government is run openly and there is no abuse of power or authority.
- The government is held accountable and its decision-making is checked for corruption or wrongdoing.
- The needs of the citizens are met by government – if it fails, it will be voted out at the next election.
- Freedom of information laws let the people see how resources and money are allocated and how decisions are made.
- The government makes good use of its natural, human and financial resources, to benefit the whole country.
- The functions of government are carried out efficiently by the civil service.
- The citizens have basic human rights, with freedom of expression.

Good governance also makes sure that there is little or no corruption, and that the views of minorities and of the most vulnerable are taken into account.

How to check good governance

To keep the Executive branch of government in Antigua and Barbuda in check and make sure it doesn't abuse its powers, some institutions have been set in place. These include:

- **Auditor General:** this person is responsible for keeping a close check on the collection and spending of public funds, to make sure they are spent correctly.

- **Ombudsman/woman:** this person is responsible for checking day-to-day operations of the ministries, tax offices, licensing offices, and all other offices concerned with government business, to see if there is any corruption or inefficiency. This is done whenever there is a complaint from a citizen.

- **Attorney General:** this is the principal legal advisor to the government who is appointed by the Governor General on the advice of the Prime Minister. This person is automatically a member of Cabinet.

- **Director of Public Prosecutions (DPP):** this person can start, carry out or stop all criminal proceedings. The DPP is not subject to the control of any authority and can only be removed from office on the grounds of non-performance or mis-behaviour.

- **The Leader of the Opposition:** this person is named by the Governor General and is usually the leader of the second largest party in the House of Representatives. The main duties involve criticising and opposing controversial measures introduced by the Government.

- **The Governor General:** this person represents the king or queen of Great Britain and is appointed on the advice of the Prime Minister. They are not linked to any political party. Generally, he or she acts on the advice of the Prime Minister or the Cabinet, but may act on his or her own discretion.

- **Civil servants:** full-time employees whose duty is to serve the government of the day, loyally and effectively.

2 Citizenship

We are learning to:

- define the terms 'citizen' and 'citizenship'
- distinguish between the rights and the responsibilities of a citizen
- identify national heroes of Antigua and Barbuda
- describe the qualities of a good citizen
- explain the role of a citizen in an independent nation
- distinguish between national and personal identity.

Who is a citizen?

A citizen is someone who lives in a country and has legal rights in that country, but also has duties towards that country. Citizenship is the fact of belonging to a particular country, with the rights and responsibilities being a citizen brings.

How to become a citizen of Antigua and Barbuda

There are four ways to become a citizen of Antigua and Barbuda:

- **By birth:** When you are born in a country you automatically become its citizen. People who are born in a country are known as the indigenous people of that country.

- **By descent:** You can become a citizen of Antigua and Barbuda, without being born here, if you have a parent or grandparent who was born here. You have to prove this by sending the necessary papers to the Passport Office.

- **By registration:** Commonwealth citizens who have been living in Antigua and Barbuda legally for seven or more years can apply to become a citizen. They have to meet certain conditions.
- **By economic investment:** A person can apply to become a citizen by investing a certain amount of money into the economy of Antigua and Barbuda. It is like buying your citizenship, although you also have to meet certain conditions.

Rights and responsibilities of a citizen

As a citizen of a country, each person has rights and responsibilities. These are outlined in the country's constitution. The constitution is a written document that sets out the laws by which a country is governed.

- A **right** is a freedom that is legally protected by the constitution of the country. It is given to all persons regardless of gender, race or religion.
- A **responsibility** is something that you should do. It is a moral obligation.

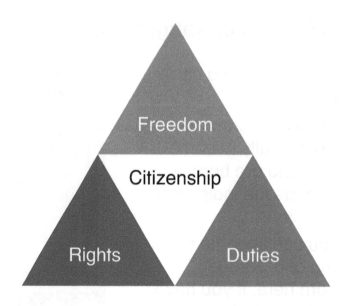

The rights of a citizen

A citizen of a country has the right to:

- be a resident in the country
- vote in free elections
- stand for public office
- be treated equally with everyone else, under the law
- be given a fair trial if accused of a crime
- enjoy the modern ideas of civil liberties, such as freedom of expression, association, movement, religion and thought.

The responsibilities of a citizen

With rights come responsibilities. As a citizen of a country a person must:

- obey the instructions of the country
- accept that the elected government has the right to rule
- pay taxes.

What makes a good citizen?

In order to be a good citizen, we need to:

- be responsible family members
- respect and obey laws
- respect the rights and properties of others
- be loyal to the nation and proud of the nation's accomplishments
- take part in community improvement activities
- use national resources wisely
- take part in government, for example, by voting and attending town hall discussions

- be well informed on important issues and willing to take a stand on those issues
- believe in equality of opportunity for all
- respect differences and way of life of others.

The role of a citizen in an independent nation

Every citizen is responsible in some way and to some extent for what happens to their country. We should respect our country and be proud to keep our country clean and respect our national symbols.

We can also participate in the decision-making process about what happens in the country by sharing our ideas and by voting to choose the person we want to represent us.

Some ways we can participate include:

- Learn as much as possible about the issues affecting the country.
- Always vote in elections.
- Join social groups, pressure groups or political parties.
- Attend community meetings or consultations.
- Take protest action when you are not pleased with a situation that is affecting you and those around you.
- Offer yourself as a candidate for political office.

If you feel that your rights are being taken away from you, what can you do? Start with a protest:

- **Marches and demonstrations** give people a chance to join with many others who share their beliefs, and is a powerful way to protest.

These workers in Greece are on strike.

- Going on **strike** is effective if your employer is treating you unfairly. It is usually done by members of a trade union. If you work in a private company, your employer will lose money. If you work for a public service, it causes a lot of disruption.

- Or you can start a **petition**. For example, you might start a petition to have a safe crossing installed outside a primary school. The more people who sign your petition the better, as it shows the strength of feeling about the matter. You then hand the petition to the people who make the decision.

If you are wrongly arrested by the police, you can claim legal compensation for any damage done as a result.

National and personal identity

Your identity is who you are – and what makes you different from everyone else.

Personal identity is the concept you have about yourself. It changes as you grow older, with the biggest change usually being as you gradually develop from being a child into an adult. It will probably include things that you have no control over, such as where you were born or the colour of your skin, but it will also reflect the choices you make in life, such as how you spend your time and what you believe.

National identity is your identity or sense of belonging to your country. It is a feeling we share with other members of the country. When we talk, we usually refer to the citizens of your country as 'we'. Unlike personal identity, it is not something we are born with, but instead is a common set of experiences or characteristics we share with our fellow citizens.

National identity is often shown in shared characteristics such as language, national colours and symbols, the history of the nation, family connections, culture, cuisine, music and heritage. Most countries have:

- a flag, an anthem and a national emblem
- a shared history and culture
- a currency (the money used in that country)
- national holidays, customs and traditions.

Coping with differences

In Antigua and Barbuda, we have a diverse culture, with citizens of different ethnicities. This can bring key differences in personal identity – and sometimes national identity, too.

As citizens of our country, we need to respect and accept these differences, and to understand that each individual is unique. Put simply, we need to be tolerant of the diversity of people, both in our local communities, and in the country as a whole.

Tolerance is the willingness to accept behaviour and beliefs that are different from your own, even though you might not agree with or approve of them.

Tolerance *is not* about accepting bad behaviour, nor about sacrificing our own beliefs. It *is* about accepting people for who they are and treating them as you would like to be treated. We should be proud of our beliefs and stand by them 100 per cent, while still celebrating the differences of others.

National heroes

A national hero is a citizen who has served his or her country very well, going above and beyond the call of duty and making significant contributions to the country. On 9 December each year, we celebrate National Heroes Day, to remember the key people who have helped make our country what it is today.

The national heroes of Antigua and Barbuda are:

Prince Klaas

Prince Klaas, also known as King Court or Tackey, was a former slave. In 1736, he organised a rebellion in the hopes of freeing all the slaves on the island. However, he was not successful as another slave gave him away and he, along with the other ringleaders, was executed.

This statue of Prince Klaas stands in St. John's.

Dame Georgiana 'Nellie' Robinson

Born on 7 December 1880, Dame Nellie was a teacher and founder of her own school, the Thomas Oliver Robinson Memorial High School. She broke down colour, class and gender barriers, believing that all children should have access to education. Dame Nellie is the country's only female hero.

Sir Vere Cornwall Bird Snr

Sir Vere Cornwall Bird Snr is known as the father and founder of the nation. He was the first Premier and the first Prime Minister. He was also one of the founding members of the Antigua Trades and Labour Union.

Sir George Herbert Walter

Sir George Walter was the second Premier of Antigua and Barbuda, from 1972 to 1976. He was head of the Progressive Labour Movement (PLM). He served the trade union and political movements for over 40 years. His contributions to the nation and in the House of Representatives have been described as being in a class of their own. One of Antigua's major highways bears his name.

Sir Lester Bryant Bird

Sir Lester served the country for over 40 years, including 18 years as Deputy Prime Minister and 10 years as Prime Minister. He was also an outstanding cricketer, footballer and athlete. Along with Sir Viv Richards, he is one of the country's two living national heroes.

Sir Isaac Vivian Alexander Richards

Sir Vivian was a West Indian cricketer considered one of the greatest batsmen of all times. He retired from Test cricket as the third most successful captain of the West Indies Team. His contribution to cricket brought great recognition to the island of Antigua and Barbuda. The country's stadium bears his name.

National heroes in other Caribbean countries include:

- **St. Kitts and Nevis:** Sir Robert Llewellyn Bradshaw
- **Saint Lucia:** Sir George Walter
- **St. Vincent and the Grenadines:** Joseph Chatoyer
- **Barbados:** Sarah-Ann Gill, Sir Frank Leslie Walcott
- **Dominica:** Cecil Rawle
- **Trinidad and Tobago:** Bertram Lloyd Marshall, Dr Stephen Bennett
- **Jamaica:** Norman Manley, Marcus Garvey

Marcus Garvey

Norman Manley

3 Agriculture

We are learning to:

- identify industries in Antigua and Barbuda, and the Caribbean
- define the term 'agriculture'
- identify the different types of agriculture in Antigua and Barbuda: commercial arable farming, small farming systems, kitchen gardens, food forests
- examine the role of agriculture in Antigua and Barbuda
- examine the impact of globalisation on agriculture in Antigua and Barbuda.

Types of industry

As a reminder, here are the four main types of industry:

- **Primary industries** involve the extraction of raw materials and natural resources from the sea and land, for example, mining, farming, fishing.
- **Secondary industries** take raw materials and natural resources and turn them into something that is useful. Examples of workers in secondary industries are factory workers, builders and carpenters.
- **Tertiary industries** involve services rather than physical goods. Examples of workers in tertiary industries are hotel workers, bus and taxi drivers, teachers, doctors, plumbers and bank workers. This sector contains the largest group of workers.
- **Quaternary industries** provide knowledge and skills, for example, scientific research and IT.

Categories of industries in Antigua and Barbuda

Types of industry that exist in Antigua and Barbuda are shown here.

Industry	Categories
Primary	Agriculture, fishing, mining, aquaculture, rearing animals
Secondary	Manufacturing: • paint • cleaning products • rum • furniture • garments Agro-processing Cottage industries
Tertiary	Tourism, offshore financial services

Industries across the Caribbean

Most countries in the Caribbean have tourism as the main industry, like Antigua, but some still earn significant money from agriculture. The following table shows the main industries of Caribbean islands.

Island	Main industries
Dominica	Agriculture, tourism, manufacturing
Grenada	Tourism, agriculture, fishing, forestry, manufacturing
Saint Lucia	Tourism, manufacturing, agriculture
St. Kitts and Nevis	Tourism, agriculture, fishing, forestry, manufacturing
Guadeloupe	Tourism, agriculture, fishing, forestry, manufacturing
Martinique	Tourism, mining, construction
St. Vincent and the Grenadines	Agriculture, manufacturing, forestry, tourism
Anguilla	Tourism, offshore financial services, agriculture
Montserrat	Tourism, light manufacturing
Barbados	Tourism, manufacturing , agriculture
Guyana	Tourism, agriculture, manufacturing
Jamaica	Tourism, agriculture, mining, manufacturing
Trinidad and Tobago	Mining, manufacturing, tourism, construction, financing
Cuba	Tourism, agriculture, manufacturing

What is agriculture?

Agriculture involves cultivating the land, producing crops and raising livestock.

Corn growing during crop season

Agriculture was once the main industry of Antigua. Most of the island was under sugar cultivation for 300 years, although the industry gradually declined after the abolition of slavery, when plantation owners could not get the labour necessary. The industry on a large scale finally stopped in the 1960s.

Today, agriculture accounts for about 4 per cent of Antigua's economy. Tourism is now the main industry, with fishing the main industry of Barbuda.

Agriculture in Antigua and Barbuda

A farmer is a person engaged in agriculture, producing food and or raw materials. Agriculture is done on both a small scale and a large scale in Antigua. Most of the farmland is located around the middle and eastern section of the island. This is because the southern side of the island has volcanic soil, while the eastern side has a mixture of soil that includes limestone. This makes it perfect for crop production.

The role of agriculture in Antigua and Barbuda

Agriculture is a major part of our lives. Without agriculture there would be no crop production or livestock management. Without crop production and livestock management we would have no meat, fruits, vegetables, milk, etc.

Agriculture is essential to provide food security – to ensure that there is basic food for the people in the country, so that no one goes hungry.

Agriculture also plays an important role in our economy, allowing for the lowering of the government's food import bill. The more food that can be produced by farmers in the country, the less money the government will have to spend outside of the country, thus enabling the government to use the money saved to improve the infrastructure of the country.

Agricultural products that Antigua and Barbuda exports

Crops are produced for local consumption and any excess is exported to other countries. Crops include bananas, coconuts, beans, carrots, cucumbers, squash, tomatoes, yams, the Antigua black pineapple and mangoes.

Antigua exports:

- fruit and vegetables to other Caribbean territories
- hot peppers and vegetables to the United Kingdom and Canada.

Pineapples and mangoes are two of Antigua's main food exports.

The official ports of entry into Antigua and Barbuda are the Deep Water Harbour in St. John and the V. C. Bird International Airport in Coolidge, St. George. These ports are used for the exporting and importing of agricultural products.

Types of agriculture

There are different types of agriculture in Antigua and Barbuda. These include:

- commercial arable farming
- small farming systems
- kitchen gardens
- food forests.

Commercial arable farming

Commercial arable farming refers to the cultivation of crops without the raising of livestock (animals). There are certain characteristics that make arable farming different from other forms of agriculture, such as the size of the farm, the type of crops, and the tools and machinery used to harvest them.

Size of farms and number of workers

Crop farms tend to cover more land than livestock farms. The number of workers needed is large and extra hired labourers are needed at certain times, such as for the harvest.

Crops grown

Many arable farms practise **monoculture** – this is the continuous growing of one crop only. This is an efficient system because it can produce more crops on the same area of land. It can, however, be harmful to the environment because it means that more fertiliser needs to be used. The Antigua black pineapple in Antigua, and sugarcane and bananas in other Caribbean countries, are examples of monoculture.

Methods

Since arable farming includes large land areas, certain kinds of machinery and equipment are necessary to plant and harvest the crop, for example, ploughs, cultivators, sprayers and choppers. For this type of farming system, large areas of land are planted and harvested at the same time.

Market prices

Another characteristic of commercial arable farming is that everything that is grown is sold at market prices, which are set by the Central Marketing Corporation. In most cases, arable farmers cannot set their own price, but instead are dependent on market prices.

In summary, commercial arable farms:

- are very large
- have many workers
- only grow one type of crop
- use machines to grow and harvest crops
- use market prices to sell crops for import and export.

Small farming systems

Small farms are more popular than arable farms in Antigua. They are characterised by an emphasis on mixed crop and animal systems – that is, plants and animals are grown together.

The farms are much smaller than arable farms. In some cases, only the farmer and his or her family are the workers. Many different types of crops are produced and animals may be reared on the same farm.

There may be some use of equipment such as a tractor and a plough. Pesticides may also be used.

Harvesting is done by hand and the crops produced are sold to customers at the public market or to supermarkets, who resell to consumers. Some farmers sell their crops directly from stalls at the side of the road, or on the farm itself.

One type of small farming is **subsistence farming**. This is where farming is done mainly to feed the family. People who do backyard gardening can be called subsistence farmers as they are planting crops to feed themselves.

In summary, small farming systems:

- have a small land area
- do not have many workers
- grow multiple crops
- may also rear animals
- use equipment like tractor and ploughs.

Kitchen gardens

A kitchen garden is a garden where vegetables, and sometimes also fruit, are grown for personal use. This is similar to subsistence farming/ backyard gardening. Common types of crops grown in a kitchen garden include herbs and spices, used for seasoning.

A kitchen garden does not require much land or equipment. Many plants can be grown in containers and varieties of vegetables, herbs and flowers are available in smaller sizes that can be grown on patios, decks, balconies, and even windowsills.

This type of gardening is ideal for people who live in homes without access to land.

Food forests

A food forest is a system of gardening where land is saved by growing edible fruit and nut trees, vegetables and herbs in the same area.

Think of it like a house, where there are fruit and coconut trees on the upper level, while smaller plants such as vegetables, herbs and spices, as well as ornamental plants, are on the lower level. Plants such as marigolds help to control pests and other plants are used to attract insects.

An example of a food forest in Antigua and Barbuda is GreenGolds Tropical Garden in the east of the island. With four acres of land, it is home to a wide variety of plants.

With careful planning and gardening methods, a food forest can produce a great harvest of food all year round. Food forests are different from other fruit and vegetable gardens in that they are fairly self-sustaining, as well as being pesticide-free.

Agriculture: the positives and negatives

The benefits of agriculture to Antigua and Barbuda

- Agriculture provides food, both for local use and for exporting. This should lessen the country's dependence on importing food.
- The quality of the air is improved. Since crops are plants, they remove carbon dioxide from the air and release oxygen for humans and wildlife to breathe.
- The use of large areas of grassland to raise livestock helps reduce soil erosion and so reduces the risk of flooding.
- Agriculture provides us with fruits, vegetables, meat and dairy products that are full of vitamins and antioxidants, contributing to better health and disease prevention.
- Agriculture has more potential for providing jobs than other industries in Antigua and Barbuda. This is especially important when people are losing their jobs because some businesses are closing or do not provide full-time employment. Some hotels operate on a seasonal basis and so for a period of about six months persons are unemployed when these hotels close. In addition, due to the downturn in the economy some companies like Leewind Paints have closed.

Risks to agriculture on Antigua and Barbuda

- Global warming is bringing higher temperatures and more extreme weather, both of which can be damaging to crops.
- Hurricanes can wipe out entire crops, especially if they are severe. There is a threat of hurricanes every year between the months of June and November.
- There is a water shortage problem in Antigua and crops rely on water to grow well.
- Pests and possible plant diseases have to be monitored very carefully. If left untreated they may kill the crops.

- It can be difficult to attract enough people to work in agriculture.
- It is sometimes difficult to produce the right amount to meet demand. Sometimes crops are produced, but there is no market available for them, leading to wastage.

Barriers to improvement in manufacturing

One of the challenges that farmers face in the agriculture industry happens when there is a glut in the market. This is where more crops are produced than are needed by the population. If there is no manufacturing, such as agro-processing to turn these crops into something that can be used later on, they are left to waste. For example, extra mangoes could be canned, and made into jams and juices in factories. Doing this would preserve the mangoes and reduce wastage and increase revenue.

However, there are problems getting the manufacturing process to work as it should. These include:

- Lack of training: People need to be trained in how manufacturing can be done.
- Lack of machinery: The machines needed for the manufacturing process are very expensive.
- Lack of incentives to local people who want to start a manufacturing business.

Careers and employment opportunities in agriculture

The opportunities for work in agriculture are many and varied. Students with an interest in agriculture should consider the wide range of job options available, beyond the traditional careers of farming, planting or raising livestock.

Careers and employment in agriculture include:

- agricultural economist
- agricultural science teacher
- agricultural engineer
- agricultural sales representative
- agronomist
- animal nutritionist

- beekeeper
- entomologist
- extension officer
- farmer
- farm manager
- fisheries scientist
- forest ranger
- game warden
- garden shop manager
- greens keeper
- groundsman
- horticulturist
- landscaper
- loans officer
- plant pathologist
- soil scientist
- veterinary assistant
- veterinarian
- zookeeper.

The impact of globalisation on agriculture

Countries increasingly trade with each other, rather than trying to be self-sufficient, and companies operate more and more internationally. This is known as **globalisation**, and it is increasing faster all the time. With globalisation, it is becoming much harder for small countries like those in the Caribbean region to compete with larger countries. However, cooperation between Caribbean countries – in agriculture and elsewhere – can make a lot of difference:

- Agriculture can help regional integration, as countries work together sharing their ideas and expertise on crop production, for example.
- It promotes trade within the region and fosters relationships among the people.
- As well as trading among themselves, countries can pool their resources to create Caribbean products that can be traded internationally.

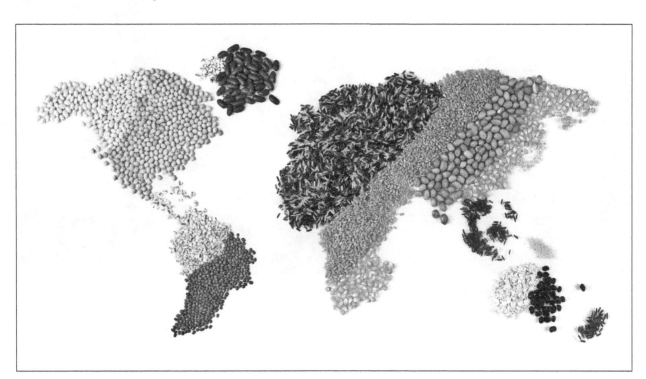

The use of technology in agriculture

As with every other industry, technology is changing the face of agriculture today.

- Farmers can use more and better machinery to help plant and harvest crops.
- They can get their crops tested for diseases through science and research.
- They can use their mobile phones to connect with other farmers, as well as with their customers.
- They can use the media to help market and sell their produce.

A vegetable hydroponic system growing cos lettuce

4 Map reading and field study

We are learning to:
- locate territories in the Caribbean
- identify lines of longitude and latitude, and coordinates
- give direction in terms of the eight-point compass
- locate a place from its latitude and longitude
- identify major land masses and oceans
- identify landforms in Antigua and Barbuda.

This chapter reviews all the map work that you have completed in the last two grades. Most of the work is practical and will be done in your Workbook.

The Caribbean region

The Caribbean region is divided into groups of islands based on geographical location. These groupings include the Antilles and the mainland territories.

The Antilles

The Antilles is divided into the Greater Antilles, the islands which bound the sea on the north, and the Lesser Antilles on the south and the east.

- The **Greater Antilles** is made up of Cuba, the Cayman Islands, Hispaniola (the Dominican Republic and Haiti), Puerto Rico and Jamaica. The Greater Antilles makes up more than 90 per cent of the land area of the West Indies.

- The **Lesser Antilles** is also known as the Caribbees. The islands form a long, partly volcanic, arc. Most of them wrap around the eastern end of the Caribbean Sea, on the western boundary with the Atlantic Ocean. A few of the islands lie on the southern fringe of the sea, just north of South America.

The Lesser Antilles is divided into the Leeward Islands and the Windward Islands.

- The **Leeward Islands** are the northern islands of the Lesser Antilles chain, starting east of Puerto Rico and running southward to Dominica. They are situated where the northeastern Caribbean Sea meets the western Atlantic Ocean.
- The **Windward Islands** are the southern islands of the Lesser Antilles. They include Dominica, Martinique, Saint Lucia, St. Vincent and the Grenadines and Grenada. Barbados and Trinidad and Tobago do not consider themselves part of the Windward Islands, but are sometimes included due to their proximity and the fact that they are windward relative to the other Caribbean islands.

The Bahamas

The Commonwealth of The Bahamas is a country consisting of 29 islands and many small rocky islets. It lies in the Atlantic Ocean north of Cuba and Hispaniola, northwest of the Turks and Caicos Islands, and southeast of the United States. It is the nearest Caribbean country to the state of Florida.

Cayman Islands

The Cayman Islands is a British Overseas Territory in the western Caribbean Sea. It is made up of three islands:

- Grand Cayman
- Cayman Brac
- Little Cayman.

Mainland territories

The mainland territories in the Caribbean are the countries that officially belong to the Caribbean, but are on the Central and South American continents, for example, Venezuela, Guyana, Suriname and French Guiana.

The Leeward Antilles

The Leeward Antilles is comprised of three islands: Aruba, Bonaire and Curaçao. They are known as the ABC islands and are located to the north of South America.

The Virgin Islands

The US and British Virgins Islands are a small group of islands located to the east of Puerto Rico. St. Croix is the largest of the US Virgin Islands.

Longitude and latitude

Lines of latitude and longitude are imaginary lines found on a map or a globe. These lines help us to give and find the exact location of places.

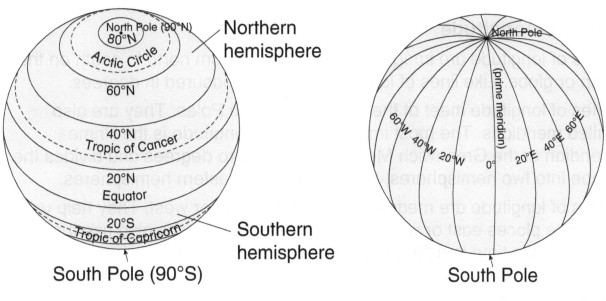

Lines of latitude

Lines of longitude

Lines of latitude

Lines of latitude run from east to west on a map or globe. They are measured in degrees north or degrees south of the Equator. The North Pole is at 90° north and the South Pole is at 90° south. There are 180 lines of latitude.

Lines of latitude help us to locate places north or south of the Equator. The Equator divides the globe into two hemispheres, the northern and southern hemispheres. Lines of latitude are also known as parallels because they never meet or touch.

The main lines of latitude you will notice on maps are the:

- Equator (0°)
- Tropic of Cancer (23.5°N)
- Tropic of Capricorn (23.5°S)
- Arctic Circle (66.5°N)
- Antarctic Circle (66.5°S)
- North Pole (90°N)
- South Pole (90°S).

Lines of longitude

Lines of longitude are imaginary lines that run from north to south on the map or globe. Like lines of latitude, they are measured in degrees.

Lines of longitude meet at the North and South Poles. They are also called meridians. The most important line of longitude is the Prime Meridian or the Greenwich Meridian. It is at zero degrees and divides the globe into two hemispheres, the eastern and western hemispheres.

Lines of longitude are measured in degrees east or west. They help us to locate places east or west of the Prime Meridian. We also use them to calculate the time in different places all over the world.

Coordinates

Where a line of latitude meets or intersects a line of longitude, a coordinate is formed. A coordinate gives us the exact location of a place on a map or globe. They are very useful for meteorologists who are tracking weather systems such as hurricanes, and for the crews of airplanes and ships who need to be able to pinpoint their exact position.

A coordinate is written using the degree for the line of latitude and longitude, for example, 20°N 80°E. The line of latitude is always written first.

Giving direction

The points of the compass are called cardinal points. There are four main ones: north, south, east and west.

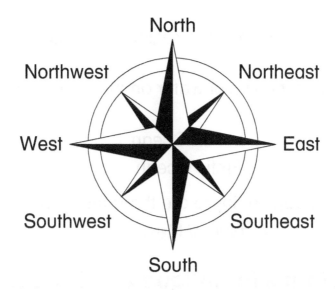

We also divide the compass further into four more directions, midway between each of the cardinal points. These are called the intermediate points: northeast, southeast, northwest and southwest.

The scale

The scale of a map shows the relationship between the distance on the map and the actual distance that it represents on the Earth. You can use a scale to calculate the actual distances on the ground.

Continents, oceans and seas

Large landmasses on the earth's surface are called continents. There are seven continents:

- North America
- South America
- Africa
- Asia

- Europe
- Australia (sometimes called Australasia to include New Zealand, or Oceania to also include other neighbouring island groups)
- Antarctica.

Central America and the Caribbean region are considered part of North America.

Oceans are the largest bodies of water on the Earth's surface. There are five oceans:

- Atlantic Ocean
- Pacific Ocean
- Indian Ocean
- Arctic Ocean
- Southern Ocean.

Within the Caribbean region, there are three main bodies of water:

- Atlantic Ocean
- Gulf of Mexico
- Caribbean Sea.

Physical landforms in Antigua and Barbuda

Here is a reminder of the principal landforms that exist in Antigua and Barbuda:

- Island – a piece of land completely surrounded by water
- Peninsula – a piece of land that is almost completely surrounded by water but is joined to a larger piece of land
- Isthmus – a narrow strip of land joining two larger pieces of land together
- Hill – a high area of land
- Mountain – a very high area of land, with steep sides
- Valley – a stretch of low land between two areas of high land
- Cave – an underground hole that can be accessed from the surface or from the sea.

Antigua is characterised by being an island with many bays and inlets around its coast. There is a high area of land in the southwest of the island, with hills, valleys and a mountain. The highest point is Mount Obama.

Barbuda is a smaller island that is mostly very flat.

5 Family

What is a family?

A family is a group of people who usually live together and are usually related to each other. This may be as parents and children, but not necessarily. Most people move away from their family of origin and form a new family once they are adult.

- The family of orientation: this is the family into which one is born. This provides children with a name, identity and a heritage. This type of family gives a child a status and locates them in the wider world.

- The family of procreation: this is where families are formed through the bearing of children. This family type is formed:

  - when a man and a woman choose to get married and have children
  - when a man and a woman choose to live together and have children without getting married.
  - by arranged marriage between two families when the parents choose the partners of their children, a marriage takes place and they have children.
  - as a result of a visiting union.

Importance of the family

Throughout history, the family has been seen as the foundation of human society. It is the core of human social life and is the most important of all social institutions. It produces a new generation, teaches the young how to behave in society, provides care and affection, regulates sexual behaviour and provides economic support.

Types of family

The main family types in the Caribbean are nuclear, single-parent, extended, sibling and blended families.

Nuclear family

A nuclear family consists of a mother, father and child or children, living together. The mother and father may be legally married or be unmarried partners.

Single-parent family

A single-parent family consists of a mother and her child/children, or a father and his child/children. One of the parents is absent. This is most commonly because the parents' partnership has broken down, but it can also be because of a deliberate choice to have a child without having a partner, because one parent has had to go away for a particular reason, or because one of the parents has died.

Extended family

An extended family usually consists of three generations of family: parents, children and grandparents. Sometimes it may include other relatives like aunts, uncles and cousins.

There are a number of ways in which an extended family may be formed:

- After a divorce, the father or mother may be forced to live with their parents for financial reasons.
- Grandparents may be unable to take care of themselves so they move in with their children and grandchildren.
- Members of the wider family choose to live together. It may help them financially, or they may just offer more support to each other.
- If a home is destroyed in a natural disaster, different family members may need to move in with relatives.

Sibling family

In a sibling family, brothers and/or sisters live together. There are no parents living in the household and the eldest sibling normally takes the role of head of the family. The situation can arise for a number of reasons, but common ones include parents leaving due to abandonment or emigration, or the parents passing away due to illness or accident.

Blended family

A blended family is created when two families come together. Both parents may have children from previous relationships that have broken down. Stepfathers, stepmothers and stepchildren are created in this type of relationship.

Foster family

A family that takes a child into their home and takes care of them is called a 'foster family'. To 'foster' means to take care of and to help develop. Foster parents may, or may not, be relatives of the child, but they are acting as parents to that child while they are living with them.

Adoptive family

An adoptive family is one that takes in another child as their own. The adoptive family takes legal responsibility for them and provides for them as if they were one of their own children.

Advantages and disadvantages of different family types

These are summarised here:

	Advantages	Disadvantages
Nuclear	The parents have the privacy and independence to raise their children as they choose. They do not need to support, or be supported by, other relatives.	They are less well supported by other relatives, who may live some distance away.
Extended	There are additional adults who can provide care and support.	The house may be overcrowded and little privacy is available for young married couples. There may be arguments about child rearing. The needs of the group outweigh the needs of the individual.
Sibling	Children learn to work together as a team. They develop a close sibling relationship. They learn to share. They learn responsibilities early.	An enormous burden is placed on the older children, who have to take the role of parents before they have learned how. It may be difficult for older children to instruct younger ones. They may experience poverty. Children do not receive the love and skills the parents could have passed on.

	Advantages	Disadvantages
Single-parent	<ul><li>Parent provides good role modelling.</li><li>The child learns independence and responsibility.</li><li>Close feeling between child and parent.</li></ul>	<ul><li>They may sometimes struggle to cope with raising children on their own as they are undertaking all the roles and tasks.</li><li>Children may miss out from not having a close relationship with the missing parent.</li><li>Parents sometimes struggle to provide financially.</li></ul>
Blended family	<ul><li>Children have more relatives to support, teach and love them.</li><li>Provides a more stable and secure life for the children.</li></ul>	<ul><li>Relationships can be difficult, with resentment and jealousies.</li><li>There may be a large number of children in the house to provide for.</li></ul>

Types of union between parents

The most common types of union between parents are:

- **Marriage:** This is a legal partnership between two adults.
- **Common-law marriage:** A couple live together as husband and wife without getting married, but they are considered to be married for social and legal purposes.
- **Visiting relationship:** This is a long-term partnership where the partners do not live together, but one visits the other from time to time. They may or may not have children.

Family tree

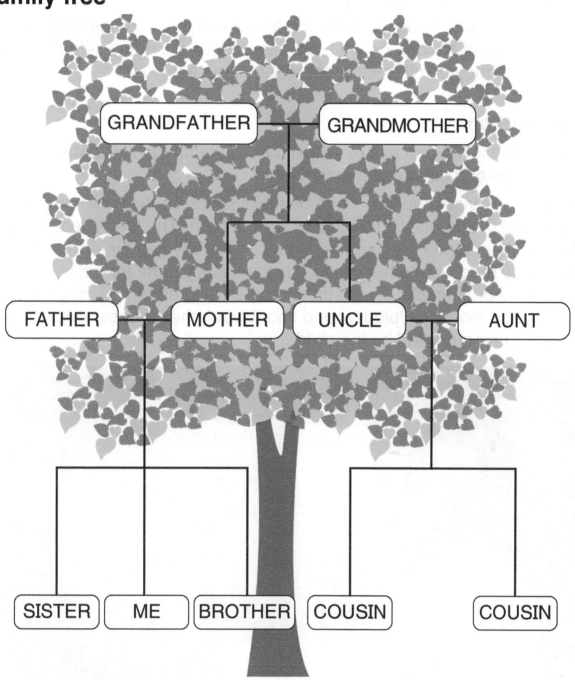

A family tree shows the relationship between members of a family for three generations or more. The oldest generation is usually at the top, going down to the youngest. One generation is usually considered to be 30 years. A grandmother, daughter and granddaughter would be three generations.

Functions of the family

Our society is largely based upon the family unit and this has been the case throughout history. As we have seen, there are many different types of family but they do all broadly serve the same functions.

Socialisation

Socialisation is the process by which children learn the roles, rules, relationships and culture of their society.

The family provides the first stage of socialisation as the family members are the first to interact with a child when it is born. The family teaches the child what the norms are and helps the child to develop their personality before they reach any other group. This is usually done through modelling. For example, if parents and older children model things like saying 'good morning', 'please' and 'thank you', then that behaviour will be copied and modelled by the child.

Reproductive function

For many years, a family unit of a mother and father was the only way in which a new generation could be created. While this is no longer the only way, it is still the most common.

Economic function

The family is the basic economic unit in many societies. The members work together as a team and jointly share in their produce. Mother and father may decide who pays which bills and who takes care of the groceries and clothing, etc. An older sibling who is working may also contribute to the family finances.

Protective function

Family members usually 'look out' for others in the family, giving them help if they are in trouble. This is most true of parents protecting children, but parents will also protect each other, as will siblings.

Status function

Parents pass on their own social identity in terms of race, ethnicity, religion, social class and culture to their children at their birth. Each individual starts out with the status of his or her family and then achieves their own when they become an adult.

The family is largely responsible for passing on the traditions, culture, customs, morals and beliefs from one generation to another.

Love and security

All humans need affection and a sense of security, and this is particularly important for children. A loving family is the best and most reliable source.

Roles of family members

Each member of a family plays their own role, which comes mostly from their position in the family. For example, a parent's role is to take care of the children and make decisions for the household.

Role of the parents

- To provide for the basic economic needs of the child
- To socialise the child so that they can fit happily into society
- To help solve the child's emotional problems.

Role of the children

- To assist parents in the home
- To do what is right (be obedient!)
- To be respectful of themselves and others.

Role of the grandparents

- To help parents with the upbringing of children
- To pass on family history and traditions
- To act as a baby sitter when the parents are busy.

Characteristics of good parenting

The job of a parent is not the easiest one, but there are some characteristics which good parents possess that will help make the job easier.

Respect

A good parent is respectful to a child even when they have to punish them. Since the family is the first stage of socialisation, children will first learn respectful behaviour from parents and guardians.

Some parents believe children should just do as they are told and not as they see the parents doing. However, this is often very unhelpful. Children who are in homes where they are treated respectfully by their parents are more likely to develop self-respect for themselves, as well as respect for others.

Listening

Good parents know how to listen more than how to talk. They provide a safe ear for children to talk to when they have problems. Most times a child does not want a parent to go and fix their problems for them. Rather, they want to know how to deal with the situation themselves. When a parent is a good listener it paves the way for open communication.

Trust

A good parent trusts their child to make decisions that are appropriate to their age. This allows the child to learn to be responsible. It also sends the message that the child can be trusted. Choices such as what movie to watch, or what to eat for dinner, can help the child learn to make more important decisions.

Leadership

A parent's main role in their child's life is as a leader, as someone that the child can model and learn from, and who will keep them healthy and safe.

Good leadership ensures that parents are firm when necessary and put rules in place even when they are unlikely to be accepted by the child. A parent who is a good leader will be aware that there are times when their children will not like them for being firm.

Courage

A good parent needs to have courage. This can show up in different ways, for example, taking an unpopular stance to instil values, rules and limits, even if it goes against the will of the child or what others believe.

Sometimes courage is needed to allow a child to make choices and experience the consequences of such choices, so that they can learn and grow.

Confidence

A good parent needs to be confident. A confident parent knows they do not have all the answers, but they are confident in their abilities to do the best they can.

If they don't know the answer, they ask for it. Confident parents are willing to accept when they are wrong, learn from it and make better choices in the future.

Gratitude

A grateful parent appreciates their child as they are. A grateful parent say to the child 'I like who you are and who you are becoming.' They focus on and accept the present moment and don't worry about the past or the future.

A parent who is grateful is approachable and is a positive influence in their child's life.

Understanding

This is the hardest characteristic for a parent to possess, but it is the one that is most needed. It can be hard for a parent to deal with a child's bad behaviour, especially when they don't understand it. However, if a child is being difficult, that is exactly when they need their parent's love the most.

Misbehaving is part of a child's growth and development, as they push the boundaries and learn what is acceptable. Understanding this will help the parent to give the child the necessary help they need in curbing negative behaviours and developing positive ones.

Happiness

Happiness does not depend on what you have or don't have, but comes from within. When a parent is happy, the home is happy and this means that the child is happy.

Patience and flexibility

Being patient does not mean tolerating bad behaviour, but if a parent loses their temper, that is the worst thing that can happen. So patience is important, as is flexibility – adapting the way you react to different children. No two children are the same.

Sense of humour

Last, but by no means least, a parent needs a sense of humour!

Family problems and social issues

Some families are not as strong as others and problems can arise. If the problems are not tackled, they can become problems for society. Such social issues are important to all of us because they affect the way we live, work and relate to one another.

Family and social issues include:

Divorce

Divorce occurs when there is a breakdown in the marriage between a man and a woman, which can happen for a number of reasons. If there appears to be no way back from the breakdown, the divorce is granted by the court according to the law and the marriage is legally terminated.

Domestic abuse

This is the wrongful treatment of one partner to the other. The abuse may be physical, verbal or mental. If the abuse is not tackled with the help of outside agencies, the results can be severe.

Child abuse

In this case, the abuse is directed at a child instead of the adult partner. If you feel you are being abused or know someone who is, you must speak to a trusted adult about it.

Teenage pregnancy

Occasionally, young girls in their teens get pregnant. They may have to drop out of school to raise the child and it will affect their life, and the life of the father for many years. This can be overwhelming, as both parents themselves are still growing up.

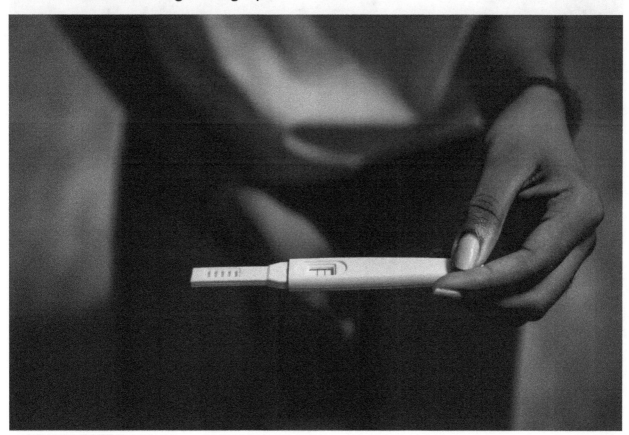

A pregnancy test

Substance abuse

Illegal drugs, such as marijuana and cocaine, as well as legal substances like alcohol, cigarettes and some over-the-counter drugs, are addictive. If family members use them, it can bring many problems.

Juvenile delinquency

Parents are a child's first teacher. Sometimes, if children lack a good example or stable home, they can fall under the influence of others who do not have their best interests in mind. These children are at risk of becoming juvenile delinquents, or criminals, who commit petty crimes such as theft and vandalism in an effort to gain money quickly or prove their bravery or strength.

Sexually-transmitted diseases

These are diseases that are passed from one person to another through sexual contact. Some are more serious than others and may be life-threatening. Sexually-transmitted diseases include gonorrhea, syphilis, HIV and Aids.

Mental illness, depression and suicide

Sometimes, people suffer from mental illnesses such as anxiety and depression. A strong and supportive family can help the person who is sick, but if left untreated it could lead to suicide, which is the wilful taking of one's own life. This act negatively affects both the individual and their family, and causes immeasurable pain for those left to mourn.

Possible solutions

The earlier issues are tackled, the more likely the intervention is to be successful. There are many possibilities but here are a few ideas:

- Education is the key way forward, for example, encouraging parents and schools to talk to young people about sexual matters and to raise awareness of the dangers of drug use.
- Stricter enforcement of the laws against substance abuse by the police.
- Publicity about the need to seek help for anyone who thinks they are the victim of abuse, or are suffering from depression or mental illness.

- Working with families where there is a breakdown in family relationships – whether between adults, possibly leading to divorce, or between adults and children.
- Developing programmes in schools where children are encouraged to talk about how they are feeling.

Laws to protect the family

Due to the many social issues that can affect the family, it becomes necessary to make laws to protect the members.

These family laws cover many different aspects of the legal system and include laws which regulate relationships within the family, such as inheritance, custody, and care of children, legal separation and divorce and domestic violence.

Family law develops and changes as a result of changing social issues and problems.

The Rights of the Child

Sometimes it is necessary to make laws to protect family members, especially children. Individual countries have their own laws regarding issues like divorce, legal separation and the care of children, but 30 years ago the United Nations Convention on the Rights of the Child came into force and has since been adopted in most countries around the world.

There are over 40 rights altogether and all countries that have signed up to the Convention are legally obliged to honour those rights. The most significant of the rights include:

- All adults must act in the best interests of the child.
- Every child has the right to live and develop healthily.
- Every child has the right to an identity – an official record of who they are.
- Children must not be separated from their parents against their will, unless it is in their best interests.
- Every child must be free to express their thoughts and opinions.
- Every child has the right to privacy.
- Every child has the right to be protected from being hurt, physically or mentally.
- Every child has the right to an education.
- Every child has the right to a standard of living that is good enough to meet their physical and social needs and support their development.

Organisations to promote healthy family relationships

Organisations in Antigua and Barbuda that help to promote healthy family relationships include:

Schools

Schools can help by educating students about the rights of the child.

Churches

Churches can help by encouraging parents to model positive behaviours, including good moral values. Doing this will help them to become good role models for their children.

Ministry of Health, Wellness and The Environment

One of the roles of this government ministry is to ensure that families are protected and taken care of. In order to do this, they provide programmes to support families who are in need. They also provide foster homes for children who are abused, as well as counselling sessions. In addition, they visit the homes of the elderly to provide care assistance to those who are living on their own.